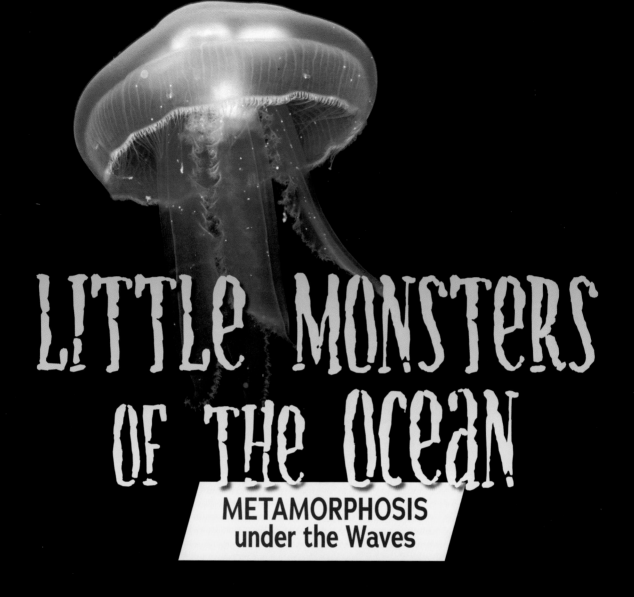

LITTLE MONSTERS OF THE OCEAN

METAMORPHOSIS under the Waves

HEATHER L. MONTGOMERY

M MILLBROOK PRESS • MINNEAPOLIS

For Kadence, may your own version of metamorphosis be miraculous!

Acknowledgments: Many scientists and citizens helped me during research, including Dr. Christopher Boyko, Dr. Lucas Brotz, Dr. Richard C. Brusca, Dr. Tom Carefoot, Dr. Susan Chiasson, Dr. J. Sook Chung, Shelly Corry, Dr. Darryl L. Felder, Dr. Adam T. Greer, Dr. Michael G. Hadfield, Dr. Carolin Haug, Dr. Nicholas Higgs, Dr. Ian Meinertzhagen, Dr. Bruce A. Menge, Dr. Anna Metaxas, Dr. Michael Miller, Dr. Mei Lin Neo, Seishoku Obata, Dr. Yuzo Ota, Dr. Gary C. B. Poore, Gar Secrist, Dr. Kaori Wakabayashi, and Tony Wu. They provided interviews, contacts, images, fact-checking, and explanations to help me understand this complex topic. Any mistakes, though, are my own.

Content Consultant: Dr. Michael G. Hadfield, Professor of Biology Emeritus, Principal Investigator Marine Invertebrate Zoology & Conservation Biology at Kewalo Marine Laboratory, University of Hawai'i at Mānoa.

Millbrook Press
A division of Lerner Publishing Group, Inc.
241 First Avenue North
Minneapolis, MN 55401 USA

For reading levels and more information, look up this title at www.lernerbooks.com.

Main body text set in Adrianna 11/16. Typeface provided by Chank.

Library of Congress Cataloging-in-Publication Data

Names: Montgomery, Heather L., author.
Title: Little monsters of the ocean : metamorphosis under the waves / Heather L. Montgomery.
Description: Minneapolis : Millbrook Press, [2019] | Audience: Age: 9–14. | Audience: Grade: 4 to 6. | Includes
    bibliographical references and index.
Identifiers: LCCN 2018016858 (print) | LCCN 2018019796 (ebook) | ISBN 9781541543812 (eb pdf) |
    ISBN 9781541528987 (lb : alk. paper)
Subjects: LCSH: Marine animals—Infancy—Juvenile literature. | Metamorphosis—Juvenile literature.
Classification: LCC QL122.2 (ebook) | LCC QL122.2 .M65 2019 (print) | DDC 591.77—dc23

LC record available at https://lccn.loc.gov/2018016858

Manufactured in the United States of America
1-44765-35702-10/15/2018

CONTENTS

Beware

This zoea is a ten-legged larva.

Gooey or grimy, spindly or spiny, monsters lurk in every ocean on Earth. They have guts to gobble venom, mucus oozing from their rear ends, and a habit of chomping on their brothers and sisters. With all that weirdness, you'd think we'd be on high alert at the beach. You'd think we'd need to protect ourselves from those creatures. Would you dare dip your toes in the ocean knowing monsters could be lurking nearby?

Instead, most of us know nothing at all about these little creatures. Yet billions of them live with us on Earth.

Why don't we know all about them?

These animals are tiny. Many are microscopic. One million could hide in 1 teaspoon (5 ml) of ocean water.

Who are these mysterious marine monsters?

They're kids!

That's right. Cute little ocean kids waiting to grow up! And as they grow, they go through some pretty dramatic changes. These changes are far more drastic than the changes you go through as you grow up—they're called metamorphosis.

You've probably heard about butterfly metamorphosis (egg, caterpillar, chrysalis, and butterfly) and frog metamorphosis (egg, tadpole, froglet, and adult). But these marine animals don't go for the kind of metamorphosis everyone has heard about. These guys go all out with their own unique take on metamorphosis. Don't take my word for it, though. See for yourself by hanging out with these little monsters for a while . . . that is, *if* you are brave enough.

MEET THE MONSTERS

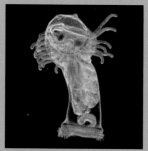

trochophore (TROK-oh-for)
plural: trochophores

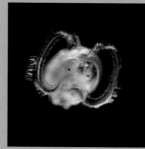

veliger (VEL-ih-jer)
plural: veligers

planula (PLAN-yuh-luh)
plural: planulae

phyllosoma (FIL-loh-SOH-muh)
plural: phyllosomas

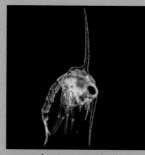

zoea (zoh-EE-uh)
plural: zoeae

gnathiid praniza (NA-thee-id prah-NIZ-uh)
plural: gnathiid praniza

CHAPTER 1

MONSTER MADNESS

What Is Metamorphosis?

Who is that spiky-headed alien? Is he going to stab you with that spike? Or whip you with his thorny tail?

No need to worry about this tyke. He's called a zoea, and he's so tiny you'd need a microscope to see him. And he's not even in control of his own body! He just wiggles around in the water, spinning in somersaults.

Why does a zoea look like a monster? Maybe that spike scares off hungry critters. He needs every bit of defense he can get. It's him against the world. And it's a rough life being little.

Even though a zoea is always searching for a meal, he has a 50 percent chance of starving to death. One reason? He can hardly swim! Zoeae are part of the plankton—organisms that drift around in the ocean without control of where they go. All they can do is suck water in and hope they slurp up something good.

But finding food isn't the only issue. Plankton often become food for other animals.

Bobbing around in the ocean, a zoea is easy prey for a striped bass with a mouth the size of a cave. One gulp and—*swish*—it's bye-bye zoea and a hundred of his buddies.

A zoea is in the first stage of life. At this point, our little guy is just a larva. He's got more growing to do. He'll grow and change and grow and change until he finally becomes a . . . blue crab!

BOY, GIRL, BOTH?

A zoea can be either a male or a female. For most marine larvae, scientists can't tell what sex they are. Some species change from male to female during their lives, while others are both female and male. In this book, the text alternates between male and female pronouns.

Blue crabs are named for their sky blue claws. Adult females have red-tipped claws. Most blue crabs are right-clawed, just like right-handed people!

TIME FOR A CHANGE

A blue crab starts life as an egg in the bay at the edge of an ocean. There, the water is shallow and warm—just right for little ones. His mother scurries around with him on her belly along with one to six million other eggs.

When he hatches, the zoea is just a thorny barb with a lot of growing to do. He doesn't look like Mom or Dad—yet. That's because he needs to go through metamorphosis. Until he does that, however, this little guy is at the mercy of the tides.

After hatching, he is washed out to sea by the tides. There, he'll spend about a month in the larval stage as a zoea, growing, growing, and growing some more. By then the zoea is huge—well, huge for a zoea—about 0.04 inches (1 mm). It's time for him to move up to the next stage, a shrimpy-looking ghost called a megalops.

A female blue crab carries her eggs on her belly. As the eggs use up their yellow yolk, they turn darker, eventually becoming black.

As a megalops, his goal is to make it back into the headwaters of the bay, where he began his life as an egg. The bay offers different kinds of food, seagrass with lots of hiding places, and not-so-salty water. But he's still just a tiny plankton—too small to swim all that way. Fortunately, now that he has morphed into a megalops, he can swim faster—up to 7.8 inches (20 cm) a second. Of course,

In the second stage of his life cycle, the megalops is easy prey. At least ninety-three different animals— bass, jellyfish, shrimp, and more—call young crabs lunch.

that's only one pencil length every second, but it might help him avoid a predator. It also might help him swim up or down to catch a current. And that current could carry him into the bay.

After his long trip back to the bay, he's tired, hungry, and ready to settle down. But he needs to be careful about where he drops down in the muck. Otherwise, he might get a nip from another crab who has gotten there first. About 75 to 97 percent of young crabs become another crabby kid's lunch. Yikes!

If a megalops avoids starving, being gobbled up, and getting washed away, his body will become wide and flat. He'll finally look like an adult, except he's only 0.08 inches (2 mm) wide, about the thickness of a nickel. That's okay. As a juvenile, he's good at growing. By the time he's one and a half years old, he'll be a full-grown adult with supersharp claws and all.

A Transformation

Metamorphosis is a process of transformation. When most people use the word, they mean the entire series of changes from a young animal (called a larva) to an adult. When most scientists use the term, they are referring to one specific change, the transformation from a larva to a juvenile (who is not yet ready to reproduce). Either way, metamorphosis can mean big changes in behavior, body structure, or the way the animal relates to the environment. A blue crab checks all three of those boxes.

During their life cycles, all animals go through phases: First, they hatch from an egg or are born. Then they have a period of growth and become adults. Lastly, they die.

megalops

zoea

juvenile

eggs

LIFE CYCLE OF A BLUE CRAB
(Images are not drawn to scale.)

mother
with eggs
(underside)

adult
(male)

Animals who undergo metamorphosis experience more extreme changes during the growth phase. They all have a larval stage that looks different from the adult stage. Think about how much a tadpole changes to become a frog or how different a caterpillar is from a butterfly. Your body changes as you grow too, but you don't grow wings. And your eye certainly doesn't move from one side of your head to the other. (A flatfish's does!)

Keep in mind, there's no right way to grow up. A butterfly's version isn't better than a blue crab's. It's just different, and it works for that creature.

But why does a crab have different stages than a butterfly? What good is metamorphosis? And what do some little ocean babies become? Keep reading! This book's got answers.

WICKED TRICKS

A crab can self-amputate! Sounds bad but if a predator is headed his way, it's an easy decision. Drop a leg as a distraction and swim away! The lucky guy can grow it back later.

CHAPTER 2

WHO MORPHS and HOW?

Metamorphosis and Molting

Frogs, flatfish, butterflies, and blue crabs all go through metamorphosis, but they aren't the only ones. Creatures on land, in the freshwater, and in the ocean experience the crazy change called metamorphosis. Believe it or not, there are more types of animals on our planet that undergo metamorphosis than ones that don't.

And every type of animal that goes through metamorphosis does it a little differently. Sometimes it's a matter of changing shapes like our little zoea. It is often also about a change in behavior, such as the flatfish who goes from swimming as a larva to living on the seafloor as an adult. A lot of other wild and wacky changes happen during metamorphosis. Some animals even need to ditch their old skin—in a process called molting—to make way for a new one. It all depends on what kind of animal they are.

Many salamanders have big bushy gills as larva but not as adults.

ANIMALS WHO MORPH

On land, many insects go through metamorphosis. A baby beetle (sometimes called a grub) is a larva that looks more like a worm than an adult insect. A beetle begins life as an egg, hatches into a larva, morphs into a pupa and, finally, becomes an adult. Plenty of other land animals such as mammals and reptiles don't go through metamorphosis. Others such as spiders and birds do change as they grow up, but because their changes are not as extreme, scientists do not consider that true metamorphosis.

Mosquito larvae hang out (literally) at the surface of the water. See the one who is right side up? That's a pupa.

A lot of insects metamorphose in freshwater too. Take a mosquito. As a larva, she lives underwater, hanging from the surface of a pond. She breathes through a snorkel that sticks out of her tail end! Mosquito larvae morph into pupae, which also hang out in the pond. The pupae don't eat, but they can do flips in the water (probably to escape from predators). After a few days, the pupa's outer covering splits and an adult comes out. Finished with metamorphosis, she flies off into the air.

Many amphibians live on land as adults but head to freshwater to lay their eggs. Salamanders go through their own version of metamorphosis. Salamander larvae grow up swimming in freshwater with big bushy gills hanging out of their necks. But most salamanders don't stay underwater forever. Just like the mosquito, the salamander larva loses her cool breathing tool when she morphs up. Some amphibians and insects go through extreme changes as they mature. By the time they are adults, they move differently, breathe differently, and hunt differently.

In the ocean, you won't find many insects or amphibians—it's just too salty for them. But there are still plenty of morphing creatures under the waves. Sea stars, clams, coral, lobsters, and some fish get in on the fun too. Any creature that is ever called a larva goes through metamorphosis. Some creatures have many other bizarre stages beyond that. To truly understand some of these wild versions of metamorphosis, you also need to understand a process called molting.

ENCASED IN ARMOR

Most animals on the planet are invertebrates—animals such as clams and crabs that don't have a backbone. And many of those invertebrates are arthropods. Arthropods include everything from shrimp to spiders and crayfish to cockroaches. They don't have backbones, but they do have jointed legs and an exoskeleton—a tough outer covering that acts like both a skeleton and a skin.

NO BONES ABOUT IT

When a hermit crab molts, she may eat her old exoskeleton to reuse the calcium.

Think about it: If your body were locked inside a suit that works like armor, wouldn't it be hard for you to grow? That's why a creature like a blue crab has to molt (shed his skeleton) every time he needs to grow larger and every time he needs to metamorphose into a new life stage.

For animals like the blue crab, molting is a part of metamorphosis. But he will also molt several times during each life stage. In the larval stage, the zoea typically has seven molts. By the time a zoea is all grown up, he will have left his skin behind twenty times!

But don't be fooled. Molting is not the same as metamorphosis. A cute little Dubois' sea snake—the most venomous sea snake in the world—molts her skin to get more room to grow, but she doesn't metamorphose. She's a reptile and not an arthropod. For arthropods, molting usually happens regularly as they grow larger. *Some* of those molts also include a radical change. *That's* metamorphosis.

There are also some animals that metamorphose but don't molt. It might be confusing to keep the difference straight. To wrap your brain around it, take a look at the life of a jellyfish.

JeLLieS DON'T MOLT

Picture an adult jellyfish. She looks like a parachute pumping her way through the water, gracefully gliding and trailing venom-tipped tentacles. But what do jellyfish kids look like?

Jellyfish larvae are called planulae. A moon jellyfish planula starts life cradled in her mother's arms. Those arms aren't like human arms. They hang from the mother's bell (the umbrella, or bell-shaped main part of her body). A bell that is covered in mucus and lined with tentacles that sting. In other words, a perfect nursery.

Once she is ready to leave Mama's arms, a planula moves out on her own. Her body is covered in tiny hairs called cilia that she beats in a wavelike pattern. The cilia act like a thousand tiny paddles, inching her forward a tiny bit. This planula may look like a yellow bundle of joy, but she's armed with venom too. She's got to take care of herself!

After a few hours or days of floating around, a planula latches onto either a rock or someone else's shell. And then the transformation into her next life stage begins. In this stage, she doesn't molt. Instead, she holds tight and grows into something that looks like a plant—a polyp.

A moon jellyfish carries venom in her tentacles.

SILLY CILIA

The word *cilia* comes from the root *cili*, Latin for "eyelid, eyelash, or a small hair." Cilia can be a single line of hairs, a tuft of hairs, or a whole surface covered in hairs. Unlike your hair, cilia don't sit still. They beat. Imagine row upon row of eyelashes all blinking together. By beating in a rhythm, cilia can either pull a creature through the water or pull water over a creature to bring in food.

The branchlike tentacles at her top snag food. A polyp is willing to eat just about anything she can get her tentacles on. If food is in short supply, she can become inactive and survive without eating for up to three years! But when food is plentiful, things get really strange. A moon jelly polyp morphs into a strobila, which looks like a polyp with a stack of saucers on top.

The saucers at her tippy top flake off one by one. Each turns into an ephyra. Phew! She sure has a lot of life stages. And she's not done yet. This *one* kid becomes two, three, ten—up to thirty ephyrae from one polyp. Weird. Especially when you find out each little swimming ephyra grows into a brand-new adult! And that is the last stage, a medusa, which we all know and love as the jellyfish.

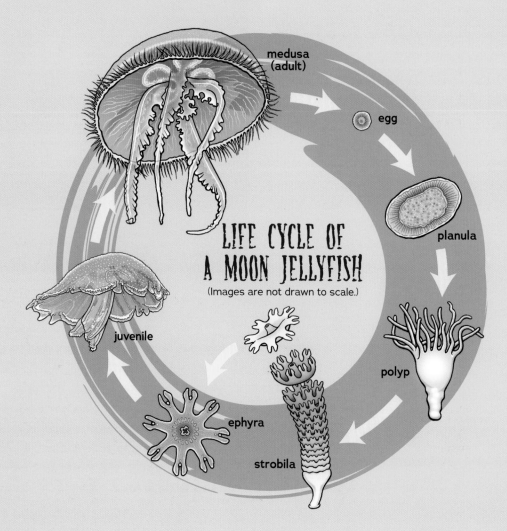

LIFE CYCLE OF A MOON JELLYFISH
(Images are not drawn to scale.)

medusa (adult)

egg

planula

polyp

strobila

ephyra

juvenile

See, a jellyfish goes through all kinds of crazy stages of metamorphosis without needing to molt. She grows, plants herself down, morphs, and flakes off layer by layer all without shedding her skin. Although her body experiences metamorphosis, she never has to molt.

Who would have thought a jellyfish transforms so much? And she's just one of many ocean creatures who does so. It's easier to spy on the metamorphosis that happens on land and in the shallows of freshwater, but many other critters metamorphose while hidden in the deep, dark ocean. There are plenty of metamorphosis mysteries left to explore.

A moon jellyfish strobila flakes off saucerlike ephyra one after the other.

COPYCAT

Moon jellyfish polyps typically copy themselves by creating platelike ephyrae. But jellyfish aren't always typical. Moon jellies can also bud off a tiny bit from their side or split themselves in half! Each of those actions can create a new polyp identical to the first one. Other jellyfish species have even more ways of copycatting themselves. Wow!

Ephyra stage of a moon jellyfish

CHAPTER 3

SURF'S UP, DUDE

Different Foods and Different Functions

A slipper lobster larva, called a phyllosoma

By now you've probably got the idea that lots (and lots) of creatures go through metamorphosis. Did you ever wonder *why* they do it?

All of that changing takes energy. Wasting energy doesn't make sense, so metamorphosis must offer some advantage to the animals who go through it. As with many mysteries of nature, scientists don't have a final answer about why. There might not even be *one* final answer. There are probably different reasons for different species.

Scientists do have some hypotheses—educated guesses backed up by evidence. One hypothesis is that metamorphosis allows larvae and adults to eat different types of food and take on different roles in the ocean. A slipper lobster might be the perfect poster child for that idea.

EaT IT!

He's got bugged-out eyes, poo packed with venom, and a habit of surfing on jellyfish. This gnarly dude is called a phyllosoma. He's the larva of a slipper lobster.

The phyllosoma is hanging loose in the surf when a jellyfish tentacle trails across him. Without wasting any time, he pokes the sharp tip of his leg in and climbs up the tentacle to the top.

Cowabunga! He's surfing!

It looks as though he's up there to catch a ride, but traveling might not be his motive. This little monster *eats* jellies.

SLIPPERY SLIMY

Jellyfish aren't completely helpless against phyllosoma. They use mucus as a weapon. The slimy stuff coats a phyllosoma. To avoid suffocation, the larva has to spend up to 50 percent of his time cleaning the gunk off.

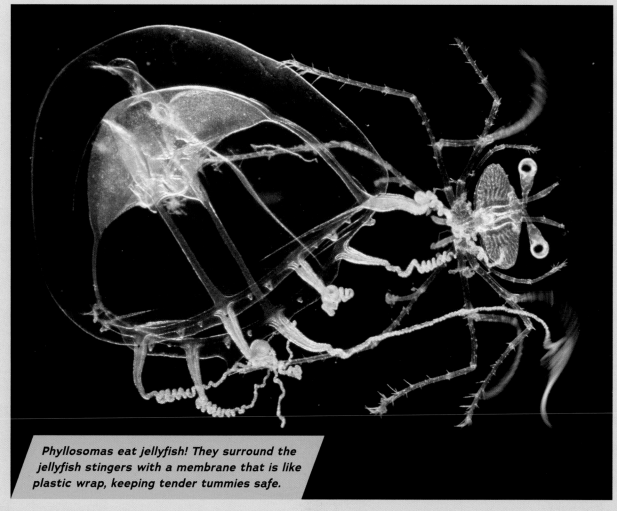

Phyllosomas eat jellyfish! They surround the jellyfish stingers with a membrane that is like plastic wrap, keeping tender tummies safe.

Radically Different

Ooey-gooey tentacles are perfect baby food—stinging cells, venom, and all. When a phyllosoma has enough of that goo to eat, he molts. After going through this process multiple times, he morphs into the next stage, a nisto. This is no minor change like getting your twelve-year molars. His front end, including his superlong legs, his head, and his stalked eyes, completely disappears! His new body is basically his old rear end.

In his new form, a nisto doesn't need to eat. For about three weeks, he lives off the energy from all that jelly goo. He can't just chill, though. He spends his time trying to find a place to settle down.

Next, he'll age up into a juvenile and start looking like an adult slipper lobster. But don't be fooled by the name. A slipper lobster is not a true lobster. As he molts, he doesn't even get claws. Instead, his head becomes a wide flat plate, perfect for slipping down into the sand. Pretty soon it'll be time for him to become Papa Slipper, and a new generation of phyllosoma will be gobbling down goo.

Do phyllosoma of all slipper species surf on jellies? Some do, but no one knows about them all. We don't have spy cams pointed at all the jellies in the ocean.

CAMO

In some species, nistos are transparent. In others, the nistos can change colors, camouflaging themselves to match their habitat.

A juvenile slipper lobster who has given up the habit of slurping jellies

My Meal

You have to admit, surfing on your dinner sounds pretty gnarly. And getting a new body has got to be radical. But what's the point of all this morphing? What are the benefits of metamorphosis to the individual and the species?

For the slipper lobster, it may be all about food. Everyone needs it, after all.

What if Mama Slipper hatched five thousand kids who all looked and acted just like her? Those kids would be crowding her space and scarfing down food—the same food she needs to eat. How would they all survive?

Survival is all about getting the resources you need. Food, water, shelter, and space—

The velvet fan lobster is a type of slipper lobster that lives off the coast of Australia.

those are all resources animals find in their habitat. Different animals can share a habitat if their resource needs don't overlap too much. Each type of animal plays a separate role or function in its habitat. Scientists call that their niche. An animal's niche is all about how it interacts with the resources. What it eats, when it eats, and how it eats, all affect the resources available to other creatures.

A mother slipper lobster lives down in the muck where she cracks open oysters, snails, and other yummy stuff. Her kids all float somewhere up above, eating gooey jellies. In other words, the mother eats food that lives on the ocean floor and the kids eat floating food. By occupying different niches at different life stages, Mama Slipper doesn't have to share her stash of snails *and* her kids get plenty of their own food.

A DOZEN EGGS?

Mother slipper lobsters carry their eggs on their abdomen. Scientists found one mother who held twenty-three thousand eggs at one time! The average number of eggs is closer to nine thousand, but not all of them hatch.

NICHE SWITCH

If you think the niches of larval and adult slipper lobsters are far apart, wait till you hear about the American eel. It's like these eels have separate dinner tables for the kids and the grown-ups—and the tables are up to 1,500 miles (2,400 km) apart! The kids live and eat in the middle of the salty sea. The others? They're way up in freshwater ponds, rivers, and streams.

You see, American eels begin their lives in the Sargasso Sea, a patch of warm water out in the North Atlantic Ocean. From that point on, they spend their lives migrating, and at each new location, their body morphs. The eggs hatch into clear, leaf-shaped larvae called leptocephali. For about a year, the leptocephali drift with the current. By the time they reach the coast of the United States, they are up to 3 inches (8 cm) long, have fins, and are called glass eels. In their next life stage, as elvers, they turn gray green. Some elvers stay along the coast. Others travel hundreds of miles up rivers. Elvers are pretty determined creatures. They'll swim up rapids, climb up dams, and even crawl out on land to get where they want to go. It may take years, but once the elvers make it upstream, they transform into yellow eels. Yellow eels swim at night and feed on insects, amphibians, and fish. That diet must be quite different from what the leptocephali ate in the ocean. After living up to forty years, the yellow eels morph into silver eels and migrate all the way back to the ocean to have kids.

Young American eels called glass eels

When it returns to the ocean, the silver eel occupies the same space as the larva. But don't worry, there isn't much competition. You see, niches aren't only about being in different places. Animals that live in the same spot can occupy different niches too. For example, one creature could like crunchy food, while the other likes squishy food. Or different niches can be about *when* they eat. But for the silver eel and the larva, it's all about what they eat. Or don't eat.

After all that metamorphosis, the silver eels don't look or act like the larva. In fact, they stop feeding entirely. To help them see in the ocean, their eyes double in size. And their guts disappear. Who needs guts if you aren't eating? The silver eel's job is to reproduce, so she fills an entirely different niche. Out in the Sargasso Sea again, the eels mate and lay eggs. What happens after that? No one knows. They probably die and become food for other fish.

An adult American eel patrols the rocky bottom of Morrison Springs cavern in Florida.

NO COMPETITION

Many ocean larvae take advantage of occupying unique niches. Queen conch babies, called veligers, whirl around the open ocean. With fingerlike flaps stretched out into the water, veligers look like miniature spaceships. Cilia on the flaps beat in waves, creating a current to pull in microscopic algae for supper.

Later, veligers settle down into the seagrass and metamorphose. They grow mouths, get gills, and lose their kiddie flaps. They still eat algae, but not the same kind. Grown-up conchs slurp along blades of seagrass and through the sand for algae. So even though kid and grown-up conchs both eat algae, they don't compete for dinner.

An adult queen conch stretches its eyes and tubelike mouth in search of algae.

Switching niches is a good deal for the whole family. Remember the zoea? Maybe that crabby kid travels to find his own niche. Different foods and functions are not the only reasons metamorphosis works well for so many creatures. Another hypothesis is that having larvae who travel can be helpful. How's that? Keep reading!

CHAPTER 4

STUCK IN THE MUD

Why Do Larvae Need to Move Around?

Did you notice that the life cycles of blue crabs, slipper lobsters, and queen conchs have a lot in common? Like most invertebrates, each of them starts as an egg and goes adventuring around the ocean during their larval stage. Then they settle down, morph into juveniles, and later become adults.

Jellyfish follow a similar pattern, except for one major difference. What's that? *When* they travel. Compare jellies to slipper lobsters. While slipper kids take a big trip in one stage of life, jellyfish juniors plop down and stay put. While slipper adults are stuck in the mud, adult jellies travel the tides.

For most marine animals, the kids get to travel. Which animals follow a similar pattern? Which ones don't? And why? Scientists have been asking those questions for a long time. The answers might depend on the lifestyle of the adults. The adults of many marine animals don't move around. So the species might need young who can travel to find new sources of food or to find mates.

A moon jellyfish medusa off the coast of Ireland

For animals who are stuck to the bottom of the ocean, metamorphosis allows an opportunity for movement. Usually it's the kids who go on an adventure. Why do jellyfish and a few other oddballs reverse the pattern? Who knows? The important thing is that they get to move around during at least one stage of their life to find a good spot to settle down. And that helps to maintain a healthy population.

An adult giant clam, all settled into the coral off the coast of Australia

BEST BUDDIES

Adult giant clams filter food out of the water, but it's not enough for those big bodies. Fortunately, friendly algae live inside the clams' tissues. Using photosynthesis, the algae make sugar from sunlight and share it with the clams. The clams provide a safe home for algae. This is a type of symbiosis called mutualism, a system through which each organism benefits.

CHAPTER 5

MOTHER KNOWS BEST

Starting Life Right

Obviously, the advantages of metamorphosis vary a lot from species to species. Another thing that varies is the amount of help larvae receive from their mothers. For every little monster in the ocean, getting a good start on life can mean the difference between life and death. So how they begin the metamorphosis process makes a big difference.

The teeny-tiny, well-fed larvae of a moon jelly drift off into the sea.

Mothers can give their young nourishment (food) and protection. There are three basic ways marine moms kick off their kids' metamorphosis: lots of nourishment, lots of eggs, or brooding.

Some mothers give their little ones lots of nourishment. They pack their large eggs with lots of yummy yolk. Before hatching, the baby uses that yolk inside the egg as food. Moon jellyfish and zombie worm moms give their kids so much yolk that once they hatch, the kids don't have to eat as larvae. That's a huge jump start on life.

But most marine mothers don't do that. Most marine mothers make lots and lots—like tens of thousands—of tiny eggs with hardly any yolk in them at all. Then they toss the eggs bye-bye into the water. Without much yolk to survive on, their kids have to hatch and find food right away or else they never will morph up to the next life stage. Blue crab, slipper lobster, and purple sea star moms do this.

And then there are a few marine mothers like the gnathiids.

Gnathiids are arthropods related to rolly pollies. A gnathiid mom broods her eggs. She carries them in a pouch like a kangaroo, except it's on her back, not her belly. Living in the sand at the bottom of the ocean, she hangs out in burrows made by worms. There, she keeps her little ones protected, safely tucked in with all their brothers and sisters.

And getting a good start is extra important for a gnathiid kid. Once he's hatched and ready to face the world, this teeny tyke has to snag a fish.

He's not okay with scarfing down a veggie diet of algae, devouring a plate of plankton, or scavenging some scraps. No, this guy is looking for something a little tastier. Something like fish blood.

This larva is a parasite—he lives off the blood or fluids of another creature. He'll latch onto a fish fin, belly, or eyeball. Then he'll stab his needlelike mouth right in, and he'll start slurping. He'll happily suck juice right out of an eye!

This kid guzzles until his belly is bulging. Once he's full of fishy goodness, he lets go. Next, he'll hang out in the mud for a while (no one knows how long) and molt. When he's hungry again, he heads off to find another fish. He'll stab, slurp, drop, and molt again. When the larva is unfed, scientists call him a zuphea. When he is fed, they call him a praniza. They think that the larva goes through this starving-feeding-molting cycle three times. Then he does more than molt. He goes through a metamorphosis.

Gnathiids: adult male (left), adult female (top right), praniza larva (bottom right)

The odd thing about an adult gnathiid is that he has huge scary jaws, but he doesn't even eat with them. Adult gnathiids don't eat *anything*. Apparently, the larvae slurp up enough to last a lifetime. What are those monster jaws for? Probably protection.

So you see, getting a good start toward finding his first meal is kind of crucial to a gnathiid larva. He really should thank his mom for all that help.

Why don't all moms brood their young? It takes a lot of energy! And toting around a bunch of kids sure slows a mama down, but it pays off if her kids survive. If eggs aren't protected, only a small percentage will make it. But brooding isn't the only option out there. Another strategy takes advantage of large numbers. Some mothers make lots of extra eggs to ensure that at least some survive.

STaR PoWeR

A purple sea star mom doesn't waste energy brooding one hundred little ones. Instead, she puts her power into making hundreds of millions of tiny eggs. Some of them meet sperm and become larvae. Sure, her larvae start their life with hardly anything, but they've got cilia. These cilia may look like no-good peach fuzz, but the little hairlike structures sweep yummy plankton into hungry mouths. Equipped with the ability to feed, the ghostly gals and guys have a chance of surviving. And survival isn't easy for a little sea star. Even finding the right food can be pretty tough. Fewer than one in a hundred make it to adulthood.

And of course, growing up is never as simple as just growing bigger. A young sea star starts

Although they are called purple sea stars, these critters can be purple, red, brown, yellow, or bright orange.

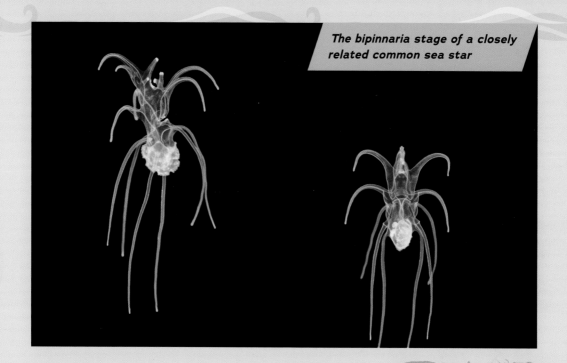

The bipinnaria stage of a closely related common sea star

as a feeding, swimming larva called a bipinnaria. Then she changes into a long-armed larva called a brachiolaria and settles to the bottom of the sea. Next, she morphs into a five-armed juvenile, and finally, she becomes an adult.

This sea star's trick—tossing out millions of eggs, which turn into little munching monsters—is pretty effective. Out of all of those eggs, someone's going to survive. Smart strategy.

COMING RIGHT UP

Sea star larvae are much more polite than their parents. Adult sea stars heave up their stomachs onto their food to digest it.

EVERYTHING THEY NEED

Golden-mouthed sea squirt mothers use a third strategy. They send their larvae off with everything they need. That way, the little squirts don't need to eat. They can focus on their job: finding a place to settle down. As adults they'll be stuck in one spot, so finding a good home is important.

The sea squirt larvae look like tiny tadpoles. But they're not frogs, toads, or any other amphibian. Sea squirts are invertebrates. And their larvae have a pretty special talent—they kill off their brains.

Huh?!

Keep reading.

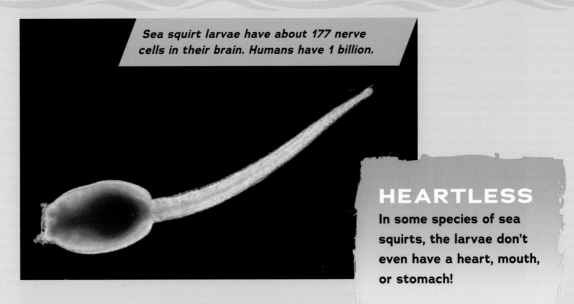

Sea squirt larvae have about 177 nerve cells in their brain. Humans have 1 billion.

HEARTLESS

In some species of sea squirts, the larvae don't even have a heart, mouth, or stomach!

These tadpole lookalikes wiggle their way through the waves, guided by their brain, which is really just a tiny group of nerve cells. With no worries about finding food, the larvae can put all their brainpower into finding a good spot to spend the rest of their lives. Once they do, it is time to metamorphose!

The larvae and the adults don't look anything alike, so this transformation requires some serious rearranging. And that requires some serious killing. No, the larvae don't kill themselves. They kill off their cells! The tips of their tails start dissolving. Their eyes, their nerve cords, and yes, even their teeny-tiny brains get broken into bits and pieces.

As their bodies change, they grow new parts. They use the matter and energy from their younger bodies—the stuff their moms gave them—to build what they need. Soon they've got grown-up brains and their tails have completely vanished. And all those new parts? They aren't in the same spots as the old ones. What used to be their mouth end now anchors to the ocean floor. Their new mouths are where their rear ends used to be. Talk about an amazing—and kind of creepy—metamorphosis!

WHICH WAY?

So which mama knows best? Gnathiids who brood their young, sea stars who toss thousands of kids out to feed, or sea squirts who provide their little ones with enough to live off? There isn't one right answer.

Of course, none of these animals actually make decisions about how much yolk their eggs need or if they should brood their kids. A purple sea star can't suddenly start brooding eggs, and a gnathiid mom can't flip a switch and create big egg yolks. Each species is adapted to a certain way of life. A way that works for them with their own specific niches and special habitats. Moms don't have much choice about that, and kids don't have much choice about when metamorphosis will happen.

Tadpolelike larvae turn into these gold-lipped sea squirt beauties on a coral reef in Indonesia.

CHAPTER 6

GROWING UP WILD

What Controls Metamorphosis

People who harvest seafood, scientists studying marine life, and everyday inquisitive people want to know more about the process of metamorphosis. *How* does the body actually change? *How* does it know when to change? *What* controls the timing of the change? Let's explore how metamorphosis happens and how it is controlled.

To tell the truth, for many creatures, we don't know *exactly* how they do it. But scientists have spied on some little monsters enough to know a thing or two. And from that, we can make hypotheses about creatures closely related to them.

Do you remember our friend the zoea? Blue crabs have been studied a lot, so he's a great example. During his last big change, he's got to molt and metamorphose at the same time. First, he's got to loosen up his tough exoskeleton. Below the exoskeleton, a new-and-improved one grows, soft and flexible. Then the little guy gets bloated. He takes on water to swell his body like a balloon.

A spider crab zoea

Ever see someone split their pants? This kid's splitting at the seams!

The shell opens from the back, like the trunk of a car but in slow motion. Then he begins to back out. He has to tug out each body part—legs, antennae, mouth, gills, and even eye stalks—without ripping any. The only thing he leaves behind is the lining of his guts.

This blue crab (right) says bye-bye to its old exoskeleton.

Then he is free, but not really. His body is still supersoft. Without his number one defense—a tough shell—he's an easy dinner for a passing predator. Cross your fingers that he makes it!

Fortunately, that soft stuff on the outside of his body will harden into a shell. But he needs as much growing room as possible. So before his shell hardens, he's got to stretch it out. To do this he sucks in more water. It only took him thirty minutes to escape the old shell, but it will take up to six hours for this new one to harden.

Just because he's done with metamorphosis doesn't mean he's done molting. He can still grow. Depending on how big he is and how warm the water is, it might be as few as 11 days or as many as 124 days before he molts again. If everything goes right, he could live to the ripe old age of three years.

HORMONES IN CONTROL

How does a critter know when to molt and when to metamorphose? Just as you can't make a decision on when to grow, an animal doesn't think about it and decide it's time. Fortunately for crabs (and their relatives such as insects), hormones take control. Hormones are bossy little chemicals that act like messengers. One part of the body makes the hormones, and they have to travel to other parts of the body to work.

HUMAN HORMONES

Hormones control changes in the human body too. Ever had a growth spurt? Gotten a pimple? Thank your hormones.

Hormones work together or against one another to keep things under control. Some hormones are like an On switch and tell the crabby cells, "It is time to molt, molt, molt." Other hormones are like an Off switch and command, "Wait, not yet!" Scientists have found evidence of still others that give the go-ahead to metamorphose up to the next stage of life. Which hormones do which job? Just how do the hormones work together and against one another? And what triggers the hormones in the first place? Scientists are still working to solve those mysteries.

Hormones are cool and in control, but they are also slow. They need time to get to where they will be used, and then they need time to work. Meanwhile, a fellow could get gobbled up. Not every creature has time to wait around like that.

LIGHTNING SPEED

Some animals don't rely on slowpoke hormones to control their metamorphosis. Sea slugs, tube worms, and many other marine invertebrates take advantage of nerves instead. Nerves use electric impulses like miniature lightning bolts to trigger the change. Nerves can go to work fast.

You might think of slugs as slow, but when it comes to metamorphosis, sea slugs are speedy. One type of sea slug starts as a swimming, plant-eating kid-in-a-shell. It completely transforms into a sluggish, coral-eating adult-sliding-on-slime in fewer than twenty hours.

One of many types of sea slugs

That's much faster than frogs, butterflies, or crabs. Remember a zoea can take one and a half years to become a true adult. How can these slugs do such a superfast, super-drastic costume change?

A sea slug veliger drifts until it finds its favorite food—coral!

First, most of their new body parts are already waiting inside their body. They grow the parts ahead of time. Second, they skip the slow little hormones and put speedy nerves in control. It takes more than nerves, though. Young sea slugs called veligers—yep, with a name just like their relatives the conchs and clams—can't age up until they become competent. To be competent is to be ready to transform from a larva to a juvenile. It's like in a video game where you can't level up until you get the tools you need.

Once they are competent, veligers need something from their environment to flip the switches on their nerves. Something that tells them *where* to settle down.

For a sea slug, the ideal location is all about the food. Adult sea slugs are picky eaters. They won't eat anything except one kind of coral. If a veliger settles where there's no coral, it's bye-bye sea slug.

So a veliger drifts through the sea until there's evidence of yummy coral below. That evidence is a chemical that has floated up from the right coral. Usually a veliger finds a reef in three days, but if there's no coral around, a veliger can push the pause button on metamorphosis for up to seven weeks. When the kid does bump into that chemical from the coral, the chemical acts like a trigger. The veliger stops swimming and drops like a rock. It's time to settle in.

Imagine if the veliger had to wait on hormones to make this change. By the time the hormones went to work, the tide would have carried the veliger far, far away from that coral. The poor little veliger might settle down in a spot without coral, and then the slug would starve.

MORe CUeS FROM THe OUTSIDe

It turns out that all sorts of things in the environment can trigger metamorphosis. A trigger can be something chemical (such as chemicals used by the sea slug), something physical (like water temperature), or something biological (like another living being). All of those cues come from the environment, the world our little monster is swimming through.

Meet *Hydroides elegans*, a tube worm. This little larva is a cutie with button eyes and a few hairs sprouting from his head. Although he could be found in most warm, shallow harbors around the globe, he's so small you'd need a microscope to make his acquaintance.

Just like the sea slug, this larva needs something from the environment to trigger metamorphosis.

His idea of a good home is the side of a ship. How is an itty-bitty, teeny-tiny larva supposed to cruise the ocean to find a ship? Sure, he's got eyes, but they are so little. And as hard as he beats those little cilia, he is only plankton and can't swim against the current. Plus think about how big the ocean is.

Lucky for this tyke, some folks already found the perfect spot and are throwing him a welcome home party. Who? Bacteria!

Look closely at anything that's been soaking in seawater and you'll see a sticky coating of bacteria. Some parts of the ocean might have up to six thousand types of bacteria. One species of bacteria grows tails that stick up in small mounds. When a tube worm larva bumps into one of those

A tube worm larva doesn't get his tube till he grows up!

TONGUE TWISTER

The bacteria that recruits this tube worm is *Pseudoalteromonas luteoviolacea*. A fifteen-syllable name for a creature too small to be seen without a microscope!

mounds, it signals the larva that this is the perfect place to settle down. That triggers metamorphosis. His cilia fall out. Big bands of cells die off and provide the little kiddo with a tasty snack. Yum-yum. Then the larva starts creating a tube. Presto. In no time, the tube worm is all grown up in a perfectly good spot.

As it turns out, lots of other larval kids also rely on their environment for the cue to grow up.

This kid's cousins, giant tube worms, live in deep, hot vents dotted across the ocean. Down in the dark, how can they tell where those hidden vents are? The vents' heat, chemicals, or other creatures living there could provide the clue. No one's sure, yet, just which one it is.

Kid corals do this too! Many types of corals live in coral reefs among friends. Drifting along as plankton, how's the larvae to know when they are above potential BFFs? Scientists have known for years that some coral are attracted to the algae that live on coral reefs. Recently, they also discovered some coral rely on bacteria to give them a clue where to settle down.

Each and every discovery we make leads us to more questions: How many other animals depend on bacteria? What triggers the stages in each different species? How do all those hormones and nerves work?

An adult tube worm extends frilly tentacles out from a tube made of calcium.

SLIP NOT
A tube worm larva may attach himself to bacteria with a string of mucus.

CHAPTER 7

MORPHING MYSTERIES

Questions for the Future

Scientists are still swimming in a sea of questions about metamorphosis. They have general questions: Where do larvae go? What do they look like? How do they survive?

They have specific questions: How do ocean currents affect larvae? Why do some fish larvae look like invertebrate larvae? How in the world do zombie worms actually find dead whales?

And they have the most basic question of all: What is it?

Most of these questions are still unanswered. We know so little about the life cycle of many marine creatures. In a way, that's one of the most interesting things about the ocean—there is still so much to discover.

WHO ARE YOU?

In the late nineteenth century, someone pulled a little alien out of the North Sea. No one knew what it would grow into so it was called y-larva. Over one hundred years later, *still*, no one knows what it becomes!

In 2008 scientists used hormones to force y-larvae to molt. Instead of morphing into juveniles, they molted into older larvae.

Forty kinds of y-larvae have been discovered. And we don't know what *any* of them become. We've got a lot of figuring out to do.

A y-larva turns into this ypsigon, but what comes next? Who knows!

ULTIMATE HIDING PLACE

Scientists guess that y-larva adults are sluglike blobs with no eyes, mouths, or digestive tracts. They probably live *inside* some other animal!

SOLVING MYSTERIES

Don't let all those morphing mysteries give you the blues. We're getting better at tracking down clues. In the past, scientists in scuba gear could stay underwater for only short periods. Now they have underwater high-tech labs like Aquarius. Aquarius looks like a submarine with legs. It's anchored to the ocean floor beside a coral reef off the coast of Florida. Scientists can camp out in there and spy on sea life for ten days at a time.

A diver explores the sea around the underwater lab, Aquarius.

We also have cool new tools that can help us figure out morphing mysteries. Scientist Steven Morgan used floating robots to help him figure out how larvae get from place to place. The robots are made from fire extinguishers and have little fan blades that act like cilia. Like larvae, the robots can move up or down in the water, but that's about it.

The thing is, ocean currents at different water depths move at different speeds and sometimes in different directions. Could larvae take advantage of those different ocean currents like moving sidewalks? Morgan and his team used the robots to test their guess. Their results show that larvae might move up or down in the water to catch the best current to get where they need to go. Pretty cool! Maybe that's how a young blue crab gets back to the bay while he is still a little guy.

Another cool tool? Computers, of course. Scientists use special computer programs to read DNA (deoxyribonucleic acid). DNA is sort of a secret chemical code found inside cells. It gives instructions for how an animal develops and for many of its characteristics (such as what it looks like). Animals inherit their DNA—and therefore their characteristics—from their parents. So animals that are related have similar DNA. If you can crack the secret code, you will know who is related to whom.

And that's exactly what happened with *C. monstrosa*. Almost two hundred years ago, a larva was found dead in the guts of a dolphin. That larva kid couldn't tell anyone who her parents were, and scientists didn't have much to go on. Since then people occasionally found the monstrous larva, but they could still only wonder what kind of critter she became. Recently, another *C. monstrosa* larva was found in the Gulf of Mexico. A group of scientists who have been collecting DNA from ocean critters for years decided to see if they could solve the mystery. They decoded *C. monstrosa*'s DNA and found a matching code in their collection. Bingo! This little spike head turns into a kind of shrimp.

LARGEST DAILY MIGRATION ON EARTH

At night, many types of plankton swim up from the depths to feed close to the water's surface. They swim down during the day to avoid being swallowed by hungry predators.

CITIZENS HELP SCIENCE

In addition to all of those new tools, scientists have help from everyday citizens. One day a man named Seishoku Obata was on vacation in Indonesia. While scuba diving, he took a video of a crazy, clear ribbon snaking through the water. No one knew what it was. When scientist Michael Miller saw that video and some other pictures, the flared-out nose and wide-open jaw looked familiar.

Remember how American eels go through metamorphosis? They aren't the only eels to pull that stunt. Miller's team hypothesized that the clear critter was a larval ribbon eel. He shared his hypothesis with the rest of the scientific community by writing a paper about it. Is it really the larva of a ribbon eel? We probably won't know for sure until someone catches the kid and raises it into an adult or decodes the DNA. But we are getting closer to an answer.

And then there's the kickboxing peacock mantis shrimp. The adults are setting world records with their powerful punches, but of the five hundred species known, we've identified the life stages for only a few.

Humans have studied mantis shrimp for a while, but a recent breakthrough came from an unexpected place. A human kid! Some dead bodies of mantis

A peacock mantis shrimp's clublike claws can strike prey at speeds of 52 miles (83 km) per hour.

shrimp larvae had been sitting around in the Zoological Museum at the University of Copenhagen in Denmark for eighty years. In 2013 a six-year-old visiting the museum took a close look at them and noticed some different shapes. This kid discovered two new kinds of larvae! His parents, who are researchers, found two more types. WOW!

Now, which adults will those little guys become? Who knows? Maybe *you* will be the citizen scientist who figures that out.

Common types of mantis shrimp larvae

WHAT'S THE BIG DEAL?

Learning about all these morphing monsters is cool, but why is it important?

For one thing, making discoveries is a whole lot of fun. Imagine if you were the first person to watch an adult jellyfish turn back into a kid! Figuring out how things work satisfies our natural curiosity.

For another thing, people like to eat. Stir-fried slipper lobster, yum-yum. But when humans gobble without knowing much about their food, bad things can happen to animal populations. Some slipper species have started vanishing. Too many are being harvested from certain areas of the ocean. And if a species goes extinct, how might that affect other species? What about animals that eat it? Or animals that the extinct species used to eat?

Every animal has a niche to fill, a job to do. The more we know about these little monsters and the work they do, the better we can protect them. Imagine if phyllosomas weren't out there slurping up jellyfish. Jellies might overrun the ocean. Yikes! For many invertebrates, the kids' job might be even more important than the parents' job. If we eat too many mama and papa slippers before they can have more kids, who's going to tackle that jellyfish job?

Now that we know what phyllosomas eat, maybe people can grow their own slipper lobsters for supper and let the wild slippers stay wild.

Last but not least, as a part of the plankton, larvae are at the base of the ocean's food chain. To protect a big animal like a right whale, you've got to know about their food (plankton) and where the food is. If all the little larvae are on the move, the whales will move too. Knowing where the food is, thanks to those larvae-like robots, we can reroute ships so they won't crash into the whales or the larvae.

The ocean is swimming with reasons to learn about these little monsters and how they grow up. What are you waiting for? Dive in and make some of your own discoveries!

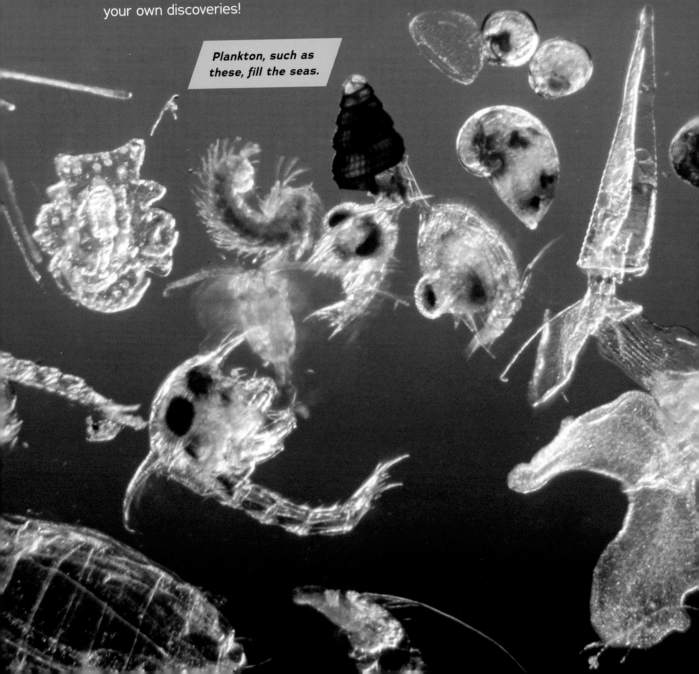

Plankton, such as these, fill the seas.

AUTHOR'S NOTE

I've always felt for the little guys—the insects, the millipedes, the crayfish. They never get as much attention as elephants, alligators, or koalas. And then there are their kids, who get even less respect. They are so small that most people don't even know they exist.

One day when I was out on a boat, we hauled up bizarre creatures from the bottom of the bay. When I learned that they were "kids," I was hooked. What were they? How did they survive? Why did they need those weirdo mouthparts? And why don't we all know about them?

Right then and there, I knew I needed to take the plunge to discover more.

I dove right into research: searching the internet, asking questions of folks I knew, and reading every book I could find on the topic (which wasn't very many). I was mesmerized by photos of the larvae but confused by all the terminology. I read college textbooks, government reports, blogs, websites, and scientific articles. I was still confused. It felt as though I was swimming through facts that didn't fit together.

In over my head, I started calling for help.

Scientists to the rescue! Scientists who study slipper lobsters, flatfish, and giant clams. Scientists like Dr. Kaori Wakabayashi from Japan, Dr. Adam Greer from Mississippi, and Dr. Mei Lin Neo from Singapore, and many others answered questions I emailed them. Those scientists were like islands in that ocean of facts. Then I discovered a life raft—Dr. Michael G. Hadfield. He's studied marine metamorphosis for decades. When I got Dr. Hadfield on the phone I had lots of "what" questions: What animals go through metamorphosis? What stages do they go through? Dr. Hadfield started talking about the "why" questions and "how" questions he had. WOW! Those big questions were really exciting and helped those facts swirling in my brain start to make sense.

That's when I realized it's okay to struggle with big questions. Even the scientists didn't have all the answers. And maybe those unanswered questions were the most exciting part of it all.

Life Stages

Whew! Keeping up with the ages and stages of these little monsters just about wore me out. So I trapped all the information in one sweet little chart for you:

CREATURE	EGG	LARVA	ADDITIONAL STAGES			ADULT
butterfly	egg	caterpillar	chrysalis			adult
frog	egg	tadpole	froglet			adult
Atlantic blue crab	egg	zoea	megalops	juvenile		adult
moon jellyfish	egg	planula	polyp	strobila	ephyra	adult
slipper lobster	egg	phyllosoma	nisto	juvenile		adult
American eel	egg	leptocephalus	glass eel	elver	yellow eel	silver eel adult
queen conch	egg	veliger				adult
zombie worm	egg	trochophore				adult
giant clam	egg	trochophore	veliger	pediveliger	juvenile	adult
gnathiid	egg	larva (zuphea, praniza)				adult
purple sea star	egg	bipinnaria, brachiolaria	juvenile			adult
golden-mouthed sea squirt	egg	larva				adult
sea slug	egg	veliger	juvenile			adult
tube worm	egg	trochophore	juvenile			adult
y-larva	egg	y-larva, ypsignon	?			adult
ribbon eel	egg	leptocephalus	?			adult
mantis shrimp	egg	larva	?			adult

GLOSSARY

amphibians: animals that live part of their life in water and part on land, such as frogs and salamanders

arthropod: a group of animals that have jointed limbs and body segments, including crabs, spiders, and centipedes

bacteria: one-celled organisms that are very simple

brood: to protect eggs until they hatch

cell: the basic unit of all life

chemical: a substance that has a specific composition

cilia: tiny hairlike structures

DNA: deoxyribonucleic acid; the substance in cells that carries information for building and maintaining a living thing

exoskeleton: an outer covering that provides both protection and structural support

gnathiid: a family of animals that are arthropods, live in the ocean, and are parasites on fish

headwaters: the beginning or source of a stream, river, or bay

hypothesis: a possible explanation based on evidence

invertebrate: an animal without a backbone

juvenile: young or not fully grown. In some species, juvenile refers to a specific life stage.

larva: an early stage in the life cycle, often the first stage after hatching

marine: of or relating to the ocean

metamorphose: to change into a different life stage

migrate: to move from one area to another for feeding or breeding

mucus: a thick, slimy fluid (such as snot) made by an animal's body

mutualism: a close relationship between organisms in which both benefit

niche: an animal's role in nature, for example, eating jellyfish so they don't become overpopulated

photosynthesis: the process by which plants make energy from light

plankton: small organisms that drift in the water

reproduction: making more organisms like oneself

species: a group of animals that are all the same type

sperm: a cell made by a male for reproduction

symbiosis: a long-term, close relationship between two organisms

vertebrate: an animal with a backbone

SELECTED BIBLIOGRAPHY

Hadfield, Michael G. Interview with the author, October 25, 2017.

Haug, Carolin, Shane T. Ahyong, Joris H. Wiethase, Jørgen Olesen, and Joachim T. Haug. "Extreme Morphologies of Mantis Shrimp Larvae." *Nauplius* 24 (2016). https://doi.org /10.1590/2358-2936e2016020.

Kerlin, Kat. "Robot Larvae Deployed at Sea." UC Davis, August 31, 2016. https://www.ucdavis.edu/news/robot-larvae-deployed-sea.

Lavalli, Kari L., and Ehud Spanier. *The Biology and Fisheries of the Slipper Lobster.* Boca Raton, FL: CRC, 2007.

Lucas, Cathy H. "Reproduction and Life History Strategies of the Common Jellyfish, *Aurelia aurita,* in Relation to Its Ambient Environment." In *Jellyfish Blooms: Ecological and Societal Importance*, edited by J. E. Purcell, W. M. Graham, and H. J. Dumont, 229–246. Dordrecht, Germany: Springer, 2001. https://doi.org/10.1007/978-94-010-0722-1_19.

Neo, Mei Lin. "Giant Clam Information." Email to the author, November 10, 2017.

Ward, George. *The Blue Crab: A Survey with Application to San Antonio Bay.* Center for Research in Water Resources, University of Texas at Austin, August 31, 2012. http://www.twdb.texas.gov/publications/reports/contracted_reports/doc /0900010973_BlueCrab.pdf.

MORE TO EXPLORE

Books

Hague, Bradley. *Alien Deep: Revealing the Mysterious Living World at the Bottom of the Ocean.* Washington, DC: National Geographic, 2012.
Explore the deepest reaches of the ocean—the hot vents—alongside scientists. Learn about an accidental discovery that changed the way we think about life at the bottom.

Johnson, Rebecca L. *Journey into the Deep: Discovering New Ocean Creatures.* Minneapolis: Millbrook Press, 2011.
Out on a boat, under the sea, or at the microscope, scientists are discovering amazing new species. From 2000 to 2010, thousands of scientists from around the world worked together to record as many marine species as possible. This book fills you in on their discoveries.

Sardet, Christian, and Mark Ohman. *Plankton: Wonders of the Drifting World.* Chicago: University of Chicago Press, 2015.
Filled with stunning photos of microscopic life, this book will suck you into the beauty and wonder of plankton. Reading it, you will learn about the origins of plankton, how plankton impacts humans, and more about the diversity of life.

Swanson, Jennifer. *Astronaut-Aquanaut: How Space Science and Sea Science Interact.* Washington, DC: National Geographic Kids, 2018.
Check out how aquanauts explore the deep ocean. Aquanauts are people who stay underwater for an extended time. Just how similar are their tools and tricks to those of astronauts?

Videos

Cnidarians: Moon Jelly Life Cycle
https://www.shapeoflife.org/video/cnidarians-moon-jelly-life-cycle
Are you wondering how a jellyfish ephyra flakes off? Watch those little flying saucers come to life!

Flatfish
https://www.youtube.com/watch?v=qePwW44HhNg
Watch a flatfish metamorphose.

Monterey Bay Aquarium Research Institute
https://www.youtube.com/channel/UCFXww6CrLAHhyZQCDnJ2g2A
See videos of marine life just doing their thing in the ocean.

Phyllosoma
https://www.youtube.com/watch?v=voQ3fKq8DMY
Don't miss this jazzy undersea look at a phyllosoma standing on a jellyfish.

Ribbon eel
https://www.youtube.com/watch?v=WQHPpqqxsto
Follow a diver who's following a ribbon eel larva.

The Secret Life of Plankton
https://www.ted.com/talks/the_secret_life_of_plankton
This informative TED video tells the story of plankton through the voice of a fish and phenomenal images.

Zooplankton Ecology Group, ICM
https://www.youtube.com/channel/UC3mZsWOvKTMDxVeZiGvevWw
This YouTube channel is full of videos of plankton—zoea, phyllosoma, and ephyra—under the microscope.

Websites

Biology of Caribbean Coral Reefs
http://www.virtualcoralreefdive.com/index.php
For a look at the biology behind coral reef creatures, plunge in!

Blue Crab Life Cycle
https://www.bluecrab.info/lifecycle.html
Here's more great stuff about the zoea and all his life stages.

Ocean Portal: Plankton and Invertebrates
http://ocean.si.edu/ocean-life-ecosystems/plankton
Use the "Ocean Life" tab and "Plankton" and "Invertebrate" links to find fun short articles.

Plantkon ID
https://planktonid.geomar.de/en
Become a citizen scientist! On this website, you can help scientists identify plankton.

Why Did the Giant Clam Cross the Road?
https://meilin5giantclam.wordpress.com/2016/05/02/why-did-the-giant-clam-cross-the-road/
Learn how scientist Mei Lin Neo spied on juvenile giant clams to discover how they walk!

INDEX

PHOTO ACKNOWLEDGMENTS

Image credits: Beliavskii Igor/Shutterstock.com (design elements); Mark Conlin/Alamy Stock Photo, p. 1; Jeffrey Hamilton/Photodisc/Getty Images, p. 2; Albert Lleal/Minden Pictures/Getty Images, p. 4; D.P. Wilson/FLPA/Science Source, pp. 5 (top left and middle bottom), 39; Dennis Kunkel Microscopy/Science Source, p. 5 (top middle); © Peter Parks/Image Quest Marine, pp. 5 (bottom left), 6, 17 (bottom), 18, 19, 20, 47; © Solvin Zankl/NPL/Minden Pictures, p. 5 (middle); Y-zo/Wikimedia Commons (CC BY-SA 3.0), pp. 5 (bottom right), 31; Yiming Chen/Moment/Getty Images, p. 7; Mdcrabwiki/Wikimedia Commons (CC-SA 3.0), p. 8; © David Eggleston/NC State University, p. 9; Laura Westlund/Independent Picture Service, pp. 10, 16, 27; Dirk Ercken/Alamy Stock Photo, p. 12; Wikimedia Commons (CC BY 2.5), p. 13; Mark Conlin/Alamy Stock Photo, p. 15; © David Wrobel/SeaPics.com, p. 17 (top); Auscape/UIG/Getty Images, p. 21; National Geographic Image Collection/Alamy Stock Photo, p. 22; © NPL/Minden Pictures, p. 23; George Karbus Photography/Cultura RF/Getty Images, p. 24; The Natural History Museum, London/Science Source, p. 25 (top); Placebo365/E/Getty Images, p. 25 (bottom); Images © Dr. Neo Mei Lin, p. 26, 28; Jupiterimages/Getty Images, p. 29; Alexander Semenov/Cultura Exclusive/Getty Images, p. 30; Sharon Eisenzopf/Shutterstock.com, p. 32; © Espen Rekdal/SeaPics.com, p. 33; © D.P. Wilson/Minden Pictures, p. 34; WaterFrame/Alamy Stock Photo, p. 34; Scenics & Science/Alamy Stock Photo, p. 36; Tony Florio/Science Source/Getty Images, p. 37; Dr. James P. McVey, NOAA Sea Grant Program - National Oceanic and Atmospheric Administration (NOAA) Central Library/Wikimedia Commons (Public Domain), p. 38; Courtesy of Dr. Michael G. Hadfield, pp. 40, 41; © Peter Parks/SeaPics.com, p. 42; AP Photo/Wilfredo Lee, p. 43; © Georgette Douwma/Minden Pictures, p. 45; Wikimedia Commons (Public Domain), p. 46; Jeffrey Hamilton/Photodisc/Getty Images, p. 48.

Cover: © Peter Parks/Image Quest Marine; Jeffrey Hamilton/Photodisc/Getty Images (claw).